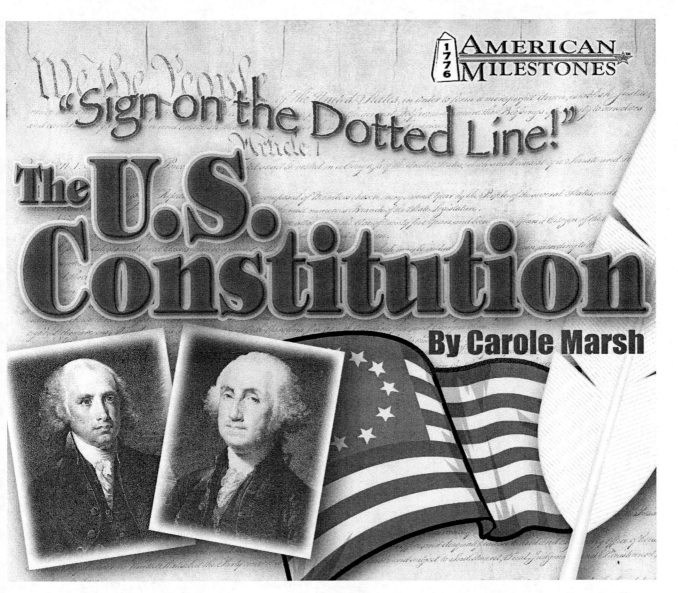

"Sign on the Dotted Line!"
The U.S. Constitution

By Carole Marsh

Editor: Chad Beard ● **Cover Design:** Michele Winkelman ● **Design & Layout:** Cecil Anderson and Lynette Rowe

Gallopade is proud to be a member of these educational organizations and associations:

The National School Supply and Equipment Association (NSSEA)
National Association for Gifted Children (NAGC)
American Booksellers Association (ABA)
Museum Store Association (MSA)
Publishers Marketing Association (PMA)
International Reading Association (IRA)
Supporter of **Association of Partners for Public Lands (APPL)**

Published by
GALLOPADE INTERNATIONAL
800-536-2GET
www.gallopade.com

D1406659

Other Carole Marsh Books

Orville & Wilbur Wright . . . Step Out Into The Sky!
Lewis & Clark Go On a Hike: The Story of the Corps of Discovery
"What A Deal!": The Louisiana Purchase
How Our Nation Was Born: The American Revolution
When Brother Fought Brother: The American Civil War
The Fight For Equality: The U.S. Civil Rights Movement
"It Can't Be Wrong!": The Bill of Rights
"Sign on the Dotted Line!": The U.S. Constitution
"Quit Bossing Us Around!": The Declaration of Independence

State Stuff™, Available for all 50 states:

My First Pocket Guide
State My First Book
State Wheel of Fortune Gamebook
State Survivor Gamebook
State Illustrated Timelines
"Jography!": A Fun Run Through Our State

The State Coloring Book
The Big Reproducible Activity Book
State Millionaire Gamebook
State Project Books
Jeopardy: Answers & Questions About
  Our State

Patriotic Favorites™

Patriotic Favorites Coloring Book
Patriotic Biographies
The Daily Patriot: 365 Quotations

Young Patriots Coloring & Activity Book
Patriotic Projects
Patriotisms: 365 Definitions

Table of Contents

Hi, I'm George Wormington. Here we go on a fascinating journey through the U.S. Constitution!

A Word From the Author

Dear Patriot,

I call you a patriot because I know you must be if you've picked up this book. Yes, I consider myself a patriot too, and like patriots before me who often misquote the French philosopher Voltaire, "I disapprove of what you say, buy I will defend to the death your right to say it." All right, maybe I won't go that far, but thank goodness for the many brave men and women in uniform who have given up their lives in order to protect our right of freedom of speech and the many other rights guaranteed us in our Constitution.

The Constitution is in some ways a living document, one that is still being debated and revised. Its wording was left intentionally vague in order to be interpreted in different ways over a period of time. Others argue that the Constitution is not a living document, but that it allows for new laws to be made as society changes.

And speaking of changes, there have been some really terrific changes made to the Constitution since it was first written. I believe that these changes were for the better. For example, the Thirteenth Amendment made slavery illegal. Another terrific change was the Nineteenth Amendment—this Amendment gave women the right to vote!

It never ceases to amaze me that the Constitution, a document more than 200 years old, has only been changed a few times since it was first signed in 1787! There are only 27 amendments to date, and the first ten were made almost right way. For the past 200 years, there have only been 17 more changes! WOW! The United States Constitution is the oldest written constitution still in use in the world. What that means is that we have a terrific Constitution!

Carole Marsh

A Timeline of Events

1776 – Declaration of Independence

1777 – Articles of Confederation endorsed by the Continental Congress and submitted to the colonies for ratification

1781 – Articles of Confederation officially "in force" after ratification by the colonies

1783 – Treaty of Paris is signed by Great Britain and the United States, ending the Revolutionary War. Senate ratifies in 1784

1786 through 1787 – Daniel Shays leads a rebellion of 1,200 men in an attack against federal arsenal in Springfield, Massachusetts—an important incident in influencing the creation of a new Constitution

1787 – Congress approves a convention to amend the Articles

1787 – Constitutional convention in Philadelphia

1787 – The Great Compromise (Connecticut Compromise) is presented by Roger Sherman, combining the Virginia and New Jersey Plans—provides for proportional representation in the House of Representatives and equal representation in the Senate

1787 – Federalist Papers begin to be published

1788 – The Constitution is in effect after receiving the approval of the requisite nine states

1789 – George Washington is elected first President of the United States—John Adams is Vice President

1791 – The Bill of Rights is ratified

"Sign on the Dotted Line!"

The U.S. Constitution

The United States had beaten Britain, and they had established a new government under the Articles of Confederation, but they were still in trouble! There was only one branch of government, the legislature, and it could not raise any military force—making it impossible to enforce any laws. There was no national executive to make important decisions, and there was no national court system to settle disputes between colonies.

"In order to form a more perfect union" something had to be done. No one wanted to sit around and lose the freedom so many had fought so hard for! When the delegates of the Constitutional Convention met, they decided that they needed a new set of rules for their government— one that would be called the U.S. Constitution.

What is the Constitution?

In May of 1787, representatives from around the country met to write a new constitution for the United States. This document replaced the old Articles of Confederation. Ideas from the Articles of Confederation as well as other earlier documents influenced the framers of the Constitution. Of the 55 representatives, 39 signed the United States Constitution on September 17, 1787. The Constitution of the United States of America, including the Bill of Rights does these things:

- Establishes the structure of the United States government

- Guarantees equality under the law with majority rule and the rights of the minority protected

- Affirms individual worth and dignity of all people

- Protects the fundamental freedoms of religion, speech, press, assembly, and petition

Fact or Opinion

A fact is something that is known to have happened or something that is known to be true. An opinion is someone's best guess, a judgement, or just simply what you think.

Read the statements below and decide whether they are fact or opinion. Write F for fact and O for opinion.

_____ 1. American constitutional government is founded on ideas expressed in earlier documents.

_____ 2. The American constitutional government is the best government in the world.

_____ 3. The Constitution encourages people to be good citizens.

_____ 4. The Constitution replaced the Articles of Confederation.

_____ 5. The Constitution establishes the structure of the United States government.

_____ 6. The Constitution affirms individual worth and dignity of all people.

_____ 7. The United States Government is a good example for other governments to follow.

Articles of Confederation

There were several reasons why the national government needed the new constitution. When the American Revolution was over, the national government had adopted the Articles of Confederation, and for a time, this document served as the nation's constitution. This document was sort of the "rule book" on how the nation was to be run. But some leaders felt that the Articles of Confederation had some problems.

The Articles of Confederation required the national legislature to have unanimous approval before they could pass any laws. This made it very difficult to get any work done because many times the states did not agree with each other.

Another reason why the new nation needed a new constitution was that even though the American Revolution was over, the new United States still faced threats from Britain and also Spain. Leaders from many states agreed that they needed to make the national government stronger in order to protect the nation.

Leaders including George Washington, Alexander Hamilton, and James Madison kept urging members of the legislature to change the Articles in order to create a stronger national government. Finally in 1787, 12 states (all but Rhode Island) had named delegates to attend the Philadelphia Convention to revise the Articles of Confederation.

True or False

Label each of these statements. Write T next to each statement that is true. Write F next to each statement that is false.

_____ 1. The Articles of Confederation were written before the U.S. Constitution.

_____ 2. The Articles of Confederation did not influence the U.S. Constitution.

_____ 3. After the American Revolution, the United States faced threats from Britain and Spain.

_____ 4. Washington, Hamilton, and Madison urged the legislature to change the Articles.

_____ 5. The Constitutional Convention was held in Washington, D.C.

_____ 6. The Constitutional Convention met in order to write the Declaration of Independence.

Constitutional Convention

Between May 25 and September 17, 1787, the Constitution of the United States was written. James Madison has often been called the Father of the Constitution. He arrived in Philadelphia for the Convention almost two weeks early so that he could start planning what they needed to get done. He kept detailed notes during the Constitutional Convention. His skills at compromise helped the delegates reach agreement during the difficult process of writing the Constitution of the United States of America.

Another founding father who played an important role at the Constitutional Convention was Benjamin Franklin. He was the oldest delegate at the convention. Franklin urged others to be willing to listen and convinced other members that compromise was important in a free society. He encouraged ratification of the Constitution and hoped that George Washington would become president of the United States under the new Constitution.

George Washington presided over the convention. He also went back to the Virginia Legislature, where he was a representative, and encouraged them to ratify the new Constitution. Eventually all of the states ratified the Constitution—but not before a lot of fussing and fighting!

Match each founding father with his description.

James Madison is called the "Father of the Constitution."

 1. Ben Franklin   2. George Washington   3. James Madison

A. "I showed up for the Constitutional Convention two weeks early."

B. "I was the oldest member at the Constitutional Convention."

C. "I presided over the Constitutional Convention."

 Elbridge Gerry, George Mason, and **Edmund Randolph** refused to sign the Constitution because they objected to the powers that the Constitution gave the federal government.

The Great Compromise

The Continental Convention was full of many delegates who knew from their own experiences why they needed a new constitution, but couldn't agree on how to make the new government work.

Delegates from many of the small states worried that they would not be fairly represented in the Congress. Delegates from the large states felt that because they had more people, they deserved to have a larger vote in the Congress. Making a compromise solved this problem.

The Connecticut delegates suggested a compromise that settled the problem. Congress would be split into two houses. Each state would have equal representation in the Senate, along with representation in proportion to population in the House of Representatives. This idea was called the Connecticut Compromise because the delegates who presented the idea were from Connecticut, but it was also called the Great Compromise.

> **WHAT IS THE CONGRESS?**
> The legislature of the United States is called the Congress. The Congress is divided into the upper house and the lower house. The upper house is called the Senate; the lower house is called the House of Representatives.

Write the cause of each effect. The first one has been done for you.

1. Effect: Delegates met at the Constitutional Convention.
   Cause: Citizens of the new United States knew they needed a new Constitution.

2. Effect: All states were given an equal vote in the Senate.
   Cause: _____

   _____

3. Effect: States were represented in the House of Representatives based on their population.
   Cause: _____

   _____

4. Effect: The Great Compromise was reached.
   Cause: _____

   _____

   _____

A total of 39 delegates signed the Constitution.

States' Rights

After the American Revolution, the new United States faced the problems of peacetime government. The states had to enforce law and order, collect taxes, pay a large public debt, and regulate trade among themselves. They also had to deal with American Indian tribes and negotiate with other governments. They needed a strong central government to help with all of these tasks.

Some of the framers of the Constitution were afraid that a powerful national government would be dangerous. They remembered what it was like living under British rule—it was difficult to get any local laws passed because the centralized government was so far away. Also, they felt that a strong national government would take power away from the states.

The Constitution established a strong central government as well as protection for the rights of the states and of every individual. The Constitution exercised authority directly over all citizens but also explained the limitations of the national government.

Color the small states red.
Color the large states blue.

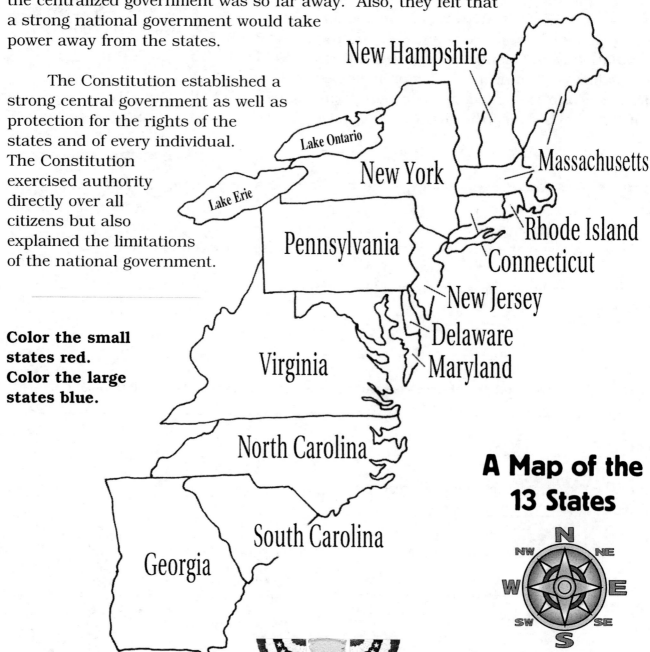

New Hampshire

Lake Ontario

New York

Massachusetts

Lake Erie

Rhode Island
Connecticut

Pennsylvania

New Jersey

Delaware
Maryland

Virginia

North Carolina

A Map of the 13 States

South Carolina

Georgia

Slavery

Slavery was a concern for many involved in framing the U.S. Constitution. Some representatives thought slavery was a bad thing that should be done away with. However, there were many representatives that were slave traders or slave owners who did not want to do away with slavery. For them the issue of slavery was not just about keeping slavery, but also whether or not slaves would be counted as part of the population.

Some members of the convention felt that slaves should not be counted as part of the population, since they did not have the same rights as citizens. On the other hand, many people felt that slaves should be counted as part of the population; after all, slaves were an important part of the economy and also provided important services such as building roads, bridges, and more. Slaves could not vote, but neither could women or most other men. The right to vote was limited to white, male, landowners who were more than 21 years old.

In order to please everybody, it was decided that representation in the Congress would be based on the free population added to three fifths of the slave population. Also Congress would not have the right to regulate the slave trade until 1808. This gave hope to some that one day, slavery would come to an end.

Pretend you are a census worker in the new United States. You have just finished counting the population of a Southern town. There are 1,063 free persons and 500 slaves. How many people will be counted for representation in the Congress?

The United States Constitution was signed September 17, 1787.

Ramble through the Preamble

The preamble of any constitution sets forth the goals and purposes of the government. The Preamble to the Constitution of the United States of America expresses the reasons why the Constitution was written. These reasons are also the purpose of the United States government.

- To form a union
- To establish justice
- To ensure domestic peace
- To provide defense

The Preamble to the Constitution of the United States of America begins, "We the people," which establishes that power of government comes from the people. This idea is also called "popular sovereignty." This means that the people rule the government and that the government does not control people.

Preamble

We the People of the United States, in Order to form a more perfect Union, establish Justice, insure domestic Tranquility, provide for the common defence, promote the general Welfare, and secure the Blessings of Liberty to ourselves and our Posterity, do ordain and establish this Constitution for the United States of America.

Put an X next to the purposes identified in the Preamble to the Constitution of the United States of America.

____ To form a union

____ To be or not to be

____ To establish justice

____ To attack other countries

____ To insure domestic peace

____ To provide defense

____ To insure foreign peace

____ To dream the impossible dream

For extra credit, use a dictionary or a thesaurus to rewrite the Preamble to the Constitution of the United States of America in your own words.

Three Branches of Government

The U.S. Constitution is like the "rule book" for how the U.S. government functions. It is the framework of the U.S. government and explains how the three branches of government work.

Legislative
● Makes laws
● Congress divided into two houses:
— Senate (2 senators per state)
— House of Representatives (number based on state population)

Judicial
● Determines if Congress' laws are constitutional
● Supreme Court

Executive
● Carries out laws
● President

Veto means "to vote against." The U.S. president has this power.

Answer the questions below.

1. Which branch of government makes laws?

_____

2. Which branch of government carries out laws?

_____

3. Which branch of government determines if laws are constitutional?

_____

The Federal System — The U.S. Constitution established the federal system of government. A federal system of government divides the power of government between national government and the governments of the states.

Checks and Balances

Separating power among the legislative, executive, and judicial branches helps prevent any one branch from abusing its power. A system of checks and balances gives each of the three branches of government ways to limit the powers of the other branches. The separation of power and checks and balances protects against an abuse of power by any one branch of the government.

LEGISLATIVE powers over
- The executive branch
— Overrides vetoes
— Impeaches a President
- The judicial branch
— Approves federal judges
— Impeaches federal judges

EXECUTIVE powers over
- The legislative branch
—Vetoes acts of Congress
— Calls Congress into special session
- The judicial branch
— Appoints federal judges

JUDICIAL powers over
- The legislative branch
—Declares laws unconstitutional
- The executive branch
— Declares executive acts unconstitutional

George Clymer, Benjamin Franklin, Robert Morris, George Read, Roger Sherman, and James Wilson also signed the Declaration of Independence.

Bill of Rights

The first ten amendments to the Constitution are also called the Bill of Rights. The Bill of Rights is part of the U.S. Constitution. The Bill of Rights is a document that describes the basic freedoms of the people of the United States. According to the Bill of Rights, the government may not violate these rights.

In the United States, people are considered to be born with certain inalienable rights—that is, rights that the government may not take away. These rights are considered to be part of a "higher law"—the idea that democracy and justice are more important than any law created by a government.

The Conventions of a number of the States having, at the time of adopting the Constitution, expressed a desire, in order to prevent misconstruction or abuse of its powers, that further declaratory and restrictive clauses should be added...

Match the rights from the Bill of Rights with an example below.

_____ 1. Freedom of speech

_____ 2. Freedom of the press

_____ 3. Right to speedy trial

_____ 4. Right to vote

_____ 5. Right to assemble

_____ 6. Freedom of religion

_____ 7. Right of trial by jury

A. You can worship as you choose

B. You don't have to spend a long time in jail before trial

C. You can go to meetings

D. A newspaper can publish people's opinions

E. You are allowed to choose your president

F. You can criticize your government

G. A group of people will decide what happens to you if you commit a crime

Why Change the Constitution?

Some framers of the Constitution would not approve it until it included a bill of rights listing the individual rights of citizens. So, the Convention promised a bill of rights would be attached to the final version. Several amendments were immediately considered when the first Congress met in 1789. Twelve amendments, written by James Madison, were presented to the states for final approval. Only ten were approved. Those ten make up the Bill of Rights. They are also the first ten amendments to the Constitution.

Including the Bill of Rights, there are 27 amendments to the Constitution. Since 1791, with the ratification of the Bill of Rights, the Constitution has only changed 17 times. That is an amazing fact considering the changes in this country in more than 200 years. The framers of the Constitution realized that no document could cover all of the changes that would take place in the world. There have been close to 10,000 amendments proposed in Congress since 1789, and only a fraction of a percentage of those receive enough support to go through the ratification process.

Here are only a few of the proposed amendments to the U.S. Constitution that were never ratified. Would you vote YES or NO on these proposed amendments?

_____ 1876 An attempt to abolish the United States Senate.

_____ 1878 An executive council of three should replace the office of president.

_____ 1893 Renaming this nation the "United States of the Earth."

_____ 1916 All acts of war should be put to a national vote. Anyone voting yes has to register as a volunteer for service in the United States Army.

_____ 1933 An attempt to limit personal wealth to $1 million.

_____ 1947 The income tax maximum for an individual should not exceed 25 percent.

_____ 1971 American citizens should have the inalienable right to an environment free of pollution.

Constitution Trivia

Enjoy Constitution trivia anywhere, anytime. See if you can answer the questions by yourself, or let everyone join in and have a lot of fun with it. Score 1 point for each correct answer. You can have a winner for each page or for the entire trivia section. Make the rules to suit the players and your time limit. Bet you laugh a lot! Bet you learn a lot!

1. Which young lieutenant colonel in the Patriot Army wrote a letter in 1780 about what he thought the country would need once the Revolutionary War was over?
    ○ a) Alexander Hamilton   ○ b) Abraham Lincoln   ○ c) Ulysses S. Grant

2. Which war brought the need for a Constitution for the new United States?
    ○ a) War Between the States   ○ b) World War I   ○ c) Revolutionary War

3. Supporters of the Constitution felt that a central government should be able to—
    ○ a) act with power, tax people, and name officers to a Cabinet.
    ○ b) invent football.
    ○ c) build cabinets.

4. Supporters of the Constitution thought that the central government should—
    ○ a) not have any Cabinet positions.
    ○ b) collect tax from the poor.
    ○ c) have more power in order to protect the nation.

Alexander Hamilton

5. The country was weak because—
    ○ a) it could not support its armies.
    ○ b) it could not pay its bills.
    ○ c) both a and b.

6. Alexander Hamilton was—
    ○ a) an aide to General George Washington.
    ○ b) not born in the United States.
    ○ c) both a and b.

7. In 1781, how many states made up the United States?
    ○ a) 3   ○ b) 48   ○ c) 13

8. In 1781, how many of the states each had their own government and constitution?
    ○ a) 3   ○ b) 48   ○ c) 13

9. Some of the founding fathers were afraid to set up a national government because—
    - ○ a) it would not be strong enough.
    - ○ b) it would be too much like France.
    - ○ c) they were afraid of losing their freedom.

10. The Constitutional Convention met in order to—
    - ○ a) rewrite the Articles of Confederation.
    - ○ b) rewrite the Declaration of Independence.
    - ○ c) rewrite the Bill of Rights.

11. The president of the Constitutional Convention was—
    - ○ a) William Shakespeare.   ○ b) George Washington.   ○ c) Benjamin Franklin.

12. Which of the following did the Constitutional Convention complete?
    - ○ a) They wrote the Declaration of Independence.
    - ○ b) They wrote the Constitution using other older documents.
    - ○ c) They declared war on Britain.

13. Which of the following was the first Constitution of the United States?
    - ○ a) Articles of Confederation
    - ○ b) Declaration of Independence
    - ○ c) neither a nor b

14. Under the Articles of Confederation, the government could—
    - ○ a) tax states   ○ b) declare war   ○ c) neither a nor b

15. When the government asked the states for money to pay the bills and soldiers, they—
    - ○ a) paid in full and proudly.
    - ○ b) paid a little bit.
    - ○ c) paid absolutely nothing.

16. To change an Article of Confederation you had to have—
    - ○ a) the vote of every state.
    - ○ b) George Washington's signature.
    - ○ c) a typewriter.

17. After the American Revolution, England had given America land—
    - ○ a) west to California and south to Florida.
    - ○ b) west to the Mississippi River and north to Canada.
    - ○ c) north to New York and south to Florida.

18. After the American Revolution, the newly independent states—
    - ○ a) were very happy with their land.
    - ○ b) fought over what belonged to whom.
    - ○ c) were ready to go back to England.

19. In the new United States, if you could not pay your bills, you were—
    - ○ a) sent to debtor's prison
    - ○ b) sent back to England
    - ○ c) both a and b

Patrick Henry

20. A Massachusetts farmer named Daniel Shays incited other poor farmers to mob the courts so judges could not send people to prison. This uprising was called—
    - ○ a) Shays' Rebellion   ○ b) the One Horse Shays   ○ c) World War I

21. James Madison, a lawyer from Virginia, called a meeting of the states to make changes in the Articles of Confederation. This meeting was called the—
    - ○ a) Continental Congress
    - ○ b) Constitutional Convention
    - ○ c) House of Parliament

22. In which city did the delegates for the Constitutional Convention meet?
    - ○ a) Philadelphia   ○ b) London   ○ c) Las Vegas

23. The men at the Constitutional Convention would come to be known as—
    - ○ a) Pennsylvanians.   ○ b) founding fathers.   ○ c) Phillies.

24. Which president of the United States did NOT attend the Continental Congress?
    - ○ a) George Washington   ○ b) James Madison   ○ c) George Bush

25. Patrick Henry was invited, but did not go, saying:
    - ○ a) "I smell a rat."
    - ○ b) "Give me liberty or give me death."
    - ○ c) "I have another engagement."

26. The Constitutional Convention was held in the Assembly Room of the Old State House in Philadelphia, now called—
    - ○ a) Congress.
    - ○ b) Printer's Alley.
    - ○ c) Independence Hall.

27. The first thing the delegates did was to—
    - ○ a) find the bathroom
    - ○ b) elect George Washington to preside
    - ○ c) ring the Liberty Bell

28. The delegates to the Constitutional Convention decided that—
    - ○ a) their meeting would be open to the public for comment.
    - ○ b) they would share every step of the decision making process with the press.
    - ○ c) everything they decided on would be kept secret until they were finished.

29. Much is known about the Constitutional Convention because—
    - ○ a) someone broke the code of secrecy.
    - ○ b) there was a spy.
    - ○ c) James Madison kept a written record.

30. The biggest argument at the Constitutional Convention was between—
    - ○ a) the big and small men.
    - ○ b) the large states and the small states.
    - ○ c) the rich and the poor.

31. On which of these plans was the Constitution of the United States based?
    - ○ a) the Virginia Plan
    - ○ b) the Pre Plan
    - ○ c) the Continental Plan

32. The Virginia Plan provided for—
    - ○ a) the nation's capital to be in Virginia.
    - ○ b) a strong national government.
    - ○ c) the Kentucky Derby.

33. The Virginia Plan called for a national executive, known today as—
    ○ a) the president.
    ○ b) a Supreme Court justice.
    ○ c) Speaker of the House.

34. Smaller states were not happy with the Virginia Plan;
    instead they presented the—
    ○ a) Small State Plan.
    ○ b) New Jersey Plan.
    ○ c) American Plan.

35. In order to decide which plan or plans to use, the delegates had heated—
    ○ a) swimming pools.   ○ b) soup.   ○ c) debates.

36. It was clear that to reach a decision, there would have to be some—
    ○ a) compromises.   ○ b) referees.   ○ c) soda crackers.

37. The Virginia Plan and the New Jersey Plan were both—
    ○ a) accepted.
    ○ b) unacceptable.
    ○ c) used to create a compromise.

38. Eventually the Connecticut delegates presented a plan that was called the—
    ○ a) Small States Compromise or the Great Compromise.
    ○ b) They're Great Compromise.
    ○ c) Connecticut Plan or the Great Compromise.

39. The Great Compromise let the House of Representatives be based on population. Which
    group of states was happy with this decision?
    ○ a) The big states   ○ b) The small states   ○ c) Southern states

40. The Senate would be elected by the state legislature. Each state would have the same
    number of Senators. This was a victory for—
    ○ a) the big states.
    ○ b) the small states.
    ○ c) Northern states.

41. The two houses—the Senate and the House of Representatives were modeled after—
   ○ a) England's House of Lords and House of Commons.
   ○ b) the House of Usher and the House that Jack built.
   ○ c) the White House and the outhouse.

42. The Senate was and still is considered—
   ○ a) the upper house.   ○ b) the middle house.   ○ c) the lower house.

43. The House of Representatives is—
   ○ a) the lower house.
   ○ b) the upper house.
   ○ c) the middle house.

44. The Constitution says that states could vote for representatives in the national government. This process is called—
   ○ a) dog eat dog.   ○ b) every man for himself.   ○ c) democracy.

45. Together, the Senate and the House of Representatives are called the—
   ○ a) White House.   ○ b) Pentagon.   ○ c) Congress.

46. According to the Constitution, the President is elected by—
   ○ a) electors.
   ○ b) Congress.
   ○ c) the elections board.

47. The Constitution established 3 branches of government called—
   ○ a) Republican, Democrat, and Independent.
   ○ b) executive, legislative, and judicial.
   ○ c) earth, wind, and fire.

48. The three branches of government provide a system of—
   ○ a) checks and balances.
   ○ b) checks and stubs.
   ○ c) checks and statements.

49. The president can veto acts of—
   ○ a) terrorism.   ○ b) Congress.   ○ c) plays.

50. The word "veto" means—
  - ○ a) to vote for.
  - ○ b) to vote against.
  - ○ c) to vote more than once.

51. Congress can impeach the president. The word impeach means—
  - ○ a) to bring formal charges against the president.
  - ○ b) to throw peaches at the president.
  - ○ c) to feed the president peach pie.

The U.S. Capitol

52. The Constitution gave Congress the power to—
  - ○ a) "provide for the common defense."
  - ○ b) "provide for the common man."
  - ○ c) "provide for the common denominator."

53. Most delegates _____ with each other.
  - ○ a) agreed
  - ○ b) disagreed
  - ○ c) could not get along

54. How long did it take to draft the final version of the Constitution (not including the Bill of Rights)?
  - ○ a) 2 years
  - ○ b) A little over 3 months
  - ○ c) 3 days

55. Who put the final version of the Constitution into proper wording?
  - ○ a) George Washington's English teacher
  - ○ b) A Committee on Style
  - ○ c) The delegates' wives

The original Constitution is on display in the National Archives Building in Washington, D.C.

Additional Resources

BOOKS

Constitution Translated For Kids by Cathy Travis, ©2002.
Published by Oakwood Publishing.
This book is a line-by-line, section-by-section simple translation of the entire U.S. Constitution. It features the actual 1787 text of the United States Constitution on the left-hand side of the page and the translation appears on the right side in the first ever side-by-side, simple translation of the short, yet most supreme, legal and political document of the United States.

The U.S. Constitution and You by Syl Sobel, ©2001.
Published by Barron's Educational Series. All elementary school students learn about the history of the U.S. Constitution when they first begin social studies. This book is different. It tells boys and girls about the great American document itself—explaining exactly what the Constitution does, as well as how it affects and protects people today.

A Kids' Guide to America's Bill of Rights: Curfews, Censorship, and the 100-Pound Giant by Kathleen Krull, ©1999. Published by Avon. Find out what the Bill of Rights is and how it affects your daily life in this fascinating look at the history, significance, and mysteries of these laws that protect the individual freedoms of everyone—even young people.

U.S. CONSTITUTION WEBSITES

http://www.constitutioncenter.org/explore/ForKids/index.shtml
http://www.archives.gov/national_archives_experience/charters/constitution.html
http://www.whitehouse.gov/kids/constitution/facts.html
http://www.socialstudiesforkids.com/subjects/constitution.htm

Glossary

amendment: a statement that is added to or improves a document (a bill or constitution etc.)

appeal: Taking a case to a higher court in order to be heard again

Bill of Rights: The first ten amendments to the United States Constitution

cabinet: A body of official advisers serving a head of state

compromise: A settlement by means of each side conceding something

confederation: An association of states

constitution: The basic law or laws of a nation or a state

Constitutional Convention: the convention of United States statesmen who drafted the United States Constitution in 1787

delegate: A person sent to represent or act for others

electors: A person authorized to vote

executive: An individual managing a nation or company

federal system: system of government with a strong central government having express powers, with some powers reserved for the states

inalienable: something that cannot be taken away

judiciary: System of courts set up to administer the law

legislature: Group of people who make and enact laws

popular sovereignty: The citizens are collectively the sovereign of the state and hold the ultimate authority over public officials and their policies.

Preamble: The opening of the Constitution that states its purpose.

ratify: To sanction officially or confirm

unanimous: in complete agreement; "a unanimous decision"

Answer Key

Page 8: 1.F; 2.O; 3.O; 4.F; 5.F; 6.F; 7.O

Page 9: 1.T; 2.F; 3.T; 4.T; 5.F; 6.F

Page 10: 1.B; 2.C; 3.A

Page 11: 2. Small states wanted to be represented equally; 3. Large states wanted to be represented based on population; 4. Large states and small states could not agree

Page 13: 1,363

Page 14: An X should appear before to form a union; to establish justice; to insure domestic peace; to provide defense

Page 15: 1. legislative; 2. executive; 3. judicial

Page 17: 1.F; 2.D; 3.B; 4.E; 5.C; 6.A; 7.G

Page 18: Answers will vary.

Page 19–25: 1.A; 2.C; 3.A; 4.C; 5.C; 6.C; 7.C; 8.C; 9.C; 10.A; 11.B; 12.B; 13.A; 14.C; 15.B; 16.A; 17.B; 18.B; 19.A; 20.A; 21.B; 22.A; 23.B; 24.C; 25.A; 26.C; 27.B; 28.C; 29.C; 30.B; 31.A; 32.B; 33.A; 34.B; 35.C; 36.A; 37.C; 38.C; 39.A; 40.B; 41.A; 42.A; 43.A; 44.C; 45.C; 46.A; 47.B; 48.A; 49.B; 50.B; 51.A; 52.A; 53.A; 54.B; 55.B

Index